GABRIELLA TEGGIA MARK HANUSZ

a cup of Java

EQUINOX
PUBLISHING
JAKARTA SINGAPORE

EQUINOX PUBLISHING (ASIA) PTE. LTD.
PO Box 6179 JKSGN
Jakarta 12062, Indonesia

www.EquinoxPublishing.com

A CUP OF JAVA

ISBN 979-95898-9-4

First Equinox Edition 2003

CONTENTS

▲ *The Java Exhibit featured glass jars with samples of coffee berries and leaves*
► *A* gamelan *orchestra in the Javanese Theater on the Midway Plaisance*
◄ *The Java Village: considered to be the most ethnological exhibit of the entire fair. Notice the newly-introduced Ferris wheel in the background.*

INTRODUCTION

The 1893 World's Columbian Exhibition, held between May and October in Chicago, was designed to celebrate the 400th anniversary of the "discovery" of America by Christopher Columbus. Countries from all over the world were invited, and 553 acres of land in central Chicago were dedicated to hosting them: there was a Donegal Castle and a Lapland Village, a Moorish Palace and a Persian Theater. It was also a platform to introduce future obsessions such as hamburgers to the United States, and a place to show off new and exciting structures like George Ferris's famous Ferris wheel.

Of all these fascinating exhibitions and product launches, one of the most popular was a massive community constructed in the middle of the fairground called the Java Village. Here were *batik* demonstrations, *wayang* and *gamelan* (puppet and music) performances – all introduced to the New World in their entirety for the first time. Inside the Java Village, a Java Lunch Room served nothing but pure Java coffee, and visitors quickly began referring to this drink as "a cup of Java".

One can imagine the exorbitant cost and logistical challenge of transporting all the performers and their equipment from the then-Netherlands East Indies. Fortunately for the performers, and for generations of coffee drinkers to come, the full cost was borne by some of the wealthiest benefactors in the Netherlands East Indies: the coffee plantations of Java. The impact of the plantations' marketing efforts was profound. Until today, the word "Java" has been synonymous with coffee.

It is well-known that the islands of Indonesia produce some of the world's finest coffee beans. Cafés from Portland to Portugal are proud to display their Estate Java, Celebes Kalossi or Sumatran Mandheling beans alongside their Jamaican Blue Mountain and Ethiopian Harrar cousins. In this book, the first in a series on Indonesian coffee varieties, we explore the history, science and significance of coffee on the island of Java. As we will see, coffee in Java is steeped in a rich past and has borne witness to nearly every social and spiritual gathering anywhere on the island. From the *kraton* to the *kampung* to the *kota*, from palace to village to town, coffee is more than just a steaming beverage – it is an integral element in the daily rituals of millions of people.

Gabriella Teggia and Mark Hanusz
Losari and Jakarta, July 2003

Leaves of the arabica coffee plant
Coffee cherries drying in the sun at the Losari Coffee Plantation in Central Java

CHAPTER ONE

JAVA COMES TO JAVA

The journey of coffee to the island of Java was long and perilous. It is a story – part legend, part fact – that has touched every continent over its almost seven-hundred-year history. Every book on coffee tells the tale of Kaldi and his goats which became hyperactive after eating coffee beans from the tree. But recent research bestows the honor of discovery on another Ethiopian, Ali bin Omar al-Shadili.

Ever since the 15th-century monk, Ali al-Shadili, drank that first cup of coffee to stay awake for evening prayers, and found that it helped induce a trance during incantations, coffee lore has inspired mysticism yet been woven into the fabric of everyday popular culture. It has been alternately revered and banned. Today coffee remains one of the world's most heavily traded commodities, at times second only to oil in value.

Arab traders were the first to recognize the value of this steaming concoction – indeed the term coffee is derived from the Ethiopian region named Kaffa. Europeans called this drink mocha: for centuries, the Yemeni port of Mocha held a monopoly on the trade of coffee beans and berries. It was the single tap from which coffee flowed to the coffeehouses of Europe, via Venice.

Coffee came to be produced on Java thanks to the cunning and entrepreneurship of the Dutch, who seized control of this precious commodity and dominated its trade for the next two hundred years.

▲ *An early 20th-century tin of Franklin's Java Coffee*
◀ *A coffee-picker on the Karangredjo Coffee Plantation near Blitar, East Java, 1925*
◀◀ *Coffee plants and workers in a cultivation garden near Sukabumi, West Java, 1924*

A Brief History of Java to Java

Almost four hundred years ago, in 1616, Pieter Van der Broeke was a young merchant for the Dutch East India Company (Vereenigde Oost-Indische Compagnie – VOC). He was wandering through the bustling trading port of Mocha on the southernmost tip of the Arabian peninsula when he stumbled upon a strange drink made from fermented beans and boiling water. While his brief was to research new trading ports, he decided this drink – called *qahwa* by the locals – was unusual enough to merit sending back to Amsterdam for analysis.

Unfortunately there was a ban – punishable by death – on the export of seedlings. All beans exported had to be boiled or roasted first so they would not germinate in any other environment. So he did what most young adventurers would have done when faced with this dilemma: he stole and then smuggled the precious seedlings aboard one of the regular VOC vessels bound for Amsterdam. On arrival he immediately brought the contraband coffee seedlings to the Amsterdam Botanical Garden where overjoyed botanists began studying their cultivation.

Around this time the merchants of Venice and Marseilles were beginning to receive regular shipments of coffee beans from Mocha. But the European buyers and Yemeni sellers were completely unaware of what was growing in the greenhouses of the Amsterdam Botanical Garden.

▲ *A trading card from one of the first companies in the United States to popularize the Mocha-Java blend, Lion Coffee of Toledo, Ohio, ca. 1890*
▶ *A chromolithograph of* Coffea arabica *from* Köhlers Medizinal-Pflanzen, *1887*
▶▶ *Collecting coffee beans on a plantation near Magelang, Central Java, ca. 1920*

3
2
1
4
7
10
8
9
A
5
6

FORNEY
CAFE
ARABICA

To Java Via India

Carolus Linnaeus, a resident botanist at the time, named the seedlings *Coffea arabica*, and kept very detailed cultivation data from his studies. He discovered that the plants would only thrive in simulated tropical conditions. The Arabs had already succeeded in growing coffee in Ceylon (now Sri Lanka), suggesting mountain air might be beneficial too. By 1658, seedlings were so well established in the Amsterdam Botanical Garden that the VOC transplanted some to Ceylon, and later to India's Malabar Coast. Emboldened by their successes in the trading of cloves and nutmeg from the Spice Islands, the VOC assumed coffee would grow just as well in the Netherlands East Indies' tropical and mountainous climate.

In 1696, the Mayor of Amsterdam, Nicholas Witsen, ordered the Dutch Commander of the Malabar Coast, Adrian Van Ommen, to take coffee seedlings from the Indian city of Cannanore and bring them to Batavia in the Netherlands East Indies. These seedlings were planted on the estate of Kedawoeng on the outskirts of Batavia, owned by Governor-General Willem van Outhoorn (1635-1720). Shortly thereafter all the seedlings were destroyed by floods. So a second batch was ordered, and reached Java the following year. This delivery fared better and by 1706 the beans from the first trial production, as well as a sample of berries and seedlings, were sent back to the Amsterdam Botanical Garden for further analysis. This coffee from Java proved to be of such

A street sign in Pondok Kopi, East Jakarta – perhaps the first coffee plantation in the Netherlands East Indies
A promotional poster for Café Arabica by Steve Forney
A forest in East Java destroyed for the Masihi Coffee Plantation, ca. 1925

B.H.MANUS.
G
A.MAYER & Co

high quality that gifts of the discovery were sent to botanical gardens around Europe. One batch given to King Louis XIV's Royal Botanical Garden was sent on to France's colonies in the West Indies, eventually reaching South and Central America. Amsterdam became so well known as a coffee trading center that Dr. James Douglas, an 18th-century scientist, regarded these plants as the ancestors of coffee plantations in the West, and named the Amsterdam Botanical Garden the "universal coffee nursery".

Botanists from the Kedawoeng Estate received approval from Amsterdam in 1710 to proceed in earnest with the cultivation of coffee. The following year 400 kilograms of prime Java coffee beans were auctioned in Amsterdam, fetching record prices. Van Outhoorn was so delighted with the commercial prospects demonstrated by the auction that he ordered the proliferation of coffee to plantations first in West Java and then further east. The VOC didn't have the human resources to manage all the plantations itself. So van Outhoorn entered into agreements with local regents under which they were compelled to grow and supply coffee exclusively to the VOC. These agreements became known as the *koffiestelsel* (coffee system) and forced growers to maintain the plantations and provide a sufficient supply of quality coffee for sale in Amsterdam. By the mid-18th century, Java coffee was considered one of the best in the world and became part of the world's oldest coffee blend, Mocha-Java.

When the VOC was dissolved in 1799, the archipelago fell under direct control of the Netherlands government and Hermann Willem Daendels (1762-1818) was appointed Governor-General in 1808. One of his first actions was to establish the Great Post Road from Anyer in the west of Java to Panarukan in the east. This was to

◂ *A Java coffee auction in Amsterdam, ca. 1930*
▸▸ *Bringing coffee beans to the Salak Estate in West Java, ca. 1929*

transport mail and troops across the island of Java – and to bring coffee from the government plantations to the port at Batavia. Coffee cultivation on Java was proving extremely productive and lucrative. And the thirst for Java coffee in Europe was unquenchable.

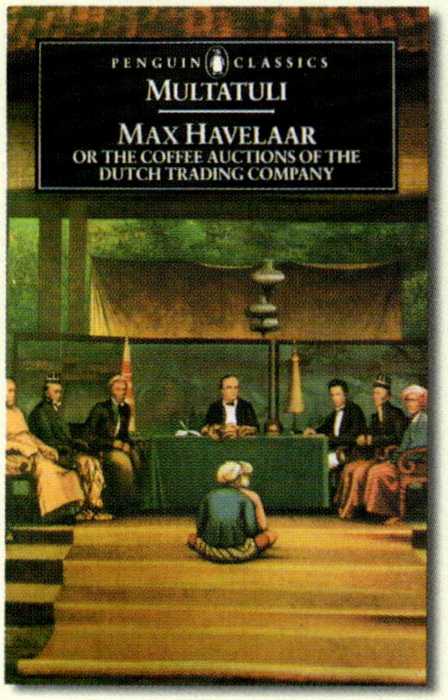

Daendels's successor, Johannes van den Bosch (1780-1844), took the *koffiestelsel* a step further and in 1830 applied it to all crops grown in the Netherlands East Indies. The *cultuurstelsel* (cultivation system) forced peasants to plant cash-crops such as sugar, indigo and coffee instead of their staple, rice. This colonial commodity fetish caused great hardship and famine across Java and Sumatra in the 1840s.

By the mid-1850s coffee production in the Netherlands East Indies had overtaken that of India and Ceylon, making Java the largest supplier of beans to the European market. Demand was great – and growing. Around this time coffeehouses were springing up all over Europe, and every bean that could be grown in the Indies was snapped up in the frantic auctions of Amsterdam.

While the *cultuurstelsel* was a success from an economic point of view, it was socially devastating for the people of what was to become Indonesia. In 1860, Eduard Douwes Dekker, under the pen name Multatuli, wrote a scathing attack on the policy of forced cultivation entitled *Max Havelaar: or The Coffee Auctions of The Dutch Trading Company.* His exposure of the cruelties and inequities imposed on the people caused moral shock and

▲ Max Havelaar, *what Indonesian novelist Pramoedya Ananta Toer called "the book that killed colonialism"*
▶ *Washing coffee at the Djati Roenggo Estate, Central Java, ca. 1925*
▶▶ *Sorting coffee beans at the Salak Estate, West Java, ca. 1929*

outrage in the Netherlands. It led to the end of the *cultuurstelsel* in 1870 with the passing of the Agrarian Reform Act. This introduced the so-called Liberal Policy which made it legal for private persons to obtain long-term land leases, fuelling the expansion of private plantations all over Java as well as Sumatra, Bali, Timor and Sulawesi. A bust of Dekker stands on a central canal bridge in Amsterdam to this day in recognition of his influence. It seemed the Netherlands East Indies would be able to maintain its near-monopoly on the finest coffee in the world. However, trouble was brewing right around the corner.

The Rust Disease

Up until the 1880s the only coffee grown in the Netherlands East Indies was arabica, considered the finest in the world. In 1878 tragedy struck, however, when every plantation across the archipelago caught the coffee blight brought on by *hemileia vasatrix*. This epidemic, called the rust disease, killed every low-lying arabica plant from Ceylon to Timor, sparing only those grown at altitudes of over one thousand meters. Crucially, this gave the Brazilians and Colombians a long-awaited opportunity to become the world's largest suppliers of arabica – a position they still hold today.

▲ *A label of the world-famous Mocha-Java blend*
◀ *Picking coffee beans on Sumatra's west coast, ca. 1925*
▶▶ *Sorting coffee beans on a plantation near Temanggung, Central Java, ca. 1929*

The plantations in the Netherlands East Indies, reeling from this disaster, scoured the world for a *Coffea* variety that would be resistant to rust disease. A solution was found in *Coffea canephora* var. *liberica*, a rougher and stronger variety that appeared immune to rust disease. While initially considered inferior to arabica, liberica was welcomed at low-lying plantations and constantly refined to a point where by 1890 it was fetching similar prices in Amsterdam's auction houses. Every low-lying plantation was back in business producing a fine cup of Java. It appeared the Netherlands East Indies would regain its position as the world's number one supplier.

By the end of the century, those hopes were dashed when the liberica plants began exhibiting a new strain of rust disease. A year later all the plants were wiped out yet again. But this time the plantations were better prepared: cultivation of a new variety from the Congo River basin called *Coffea canephora* var. *robusta* was underway. Robusta finally proved resistant to the rust disease and by 1907 had all but replaced the liberica variety on Java.

With several varieties of Java coffee on the market – arabica, liberica and robusta – competing countries took advantage of the confusion and began marketing beans as pure Java coffee. This prompted the US Department of Agriculture to rule in 1906 that only beans from the island of Java could be sold as Java coffee.

The early part of the 20th century saw the establishment of large government plantations which would be nationalized after the revolution of 1945, some held by local companies with others handed back to smallholders. Today, the Indonesian archipelago produces roughly ninety percent robusta and ten percent arabica, making Indonesia the largest producer of robusta beans in the world.

▸ *A basket full of Java robusta cherries fresh from the tree*

CHAPTER TWO

JAVA ESTATES

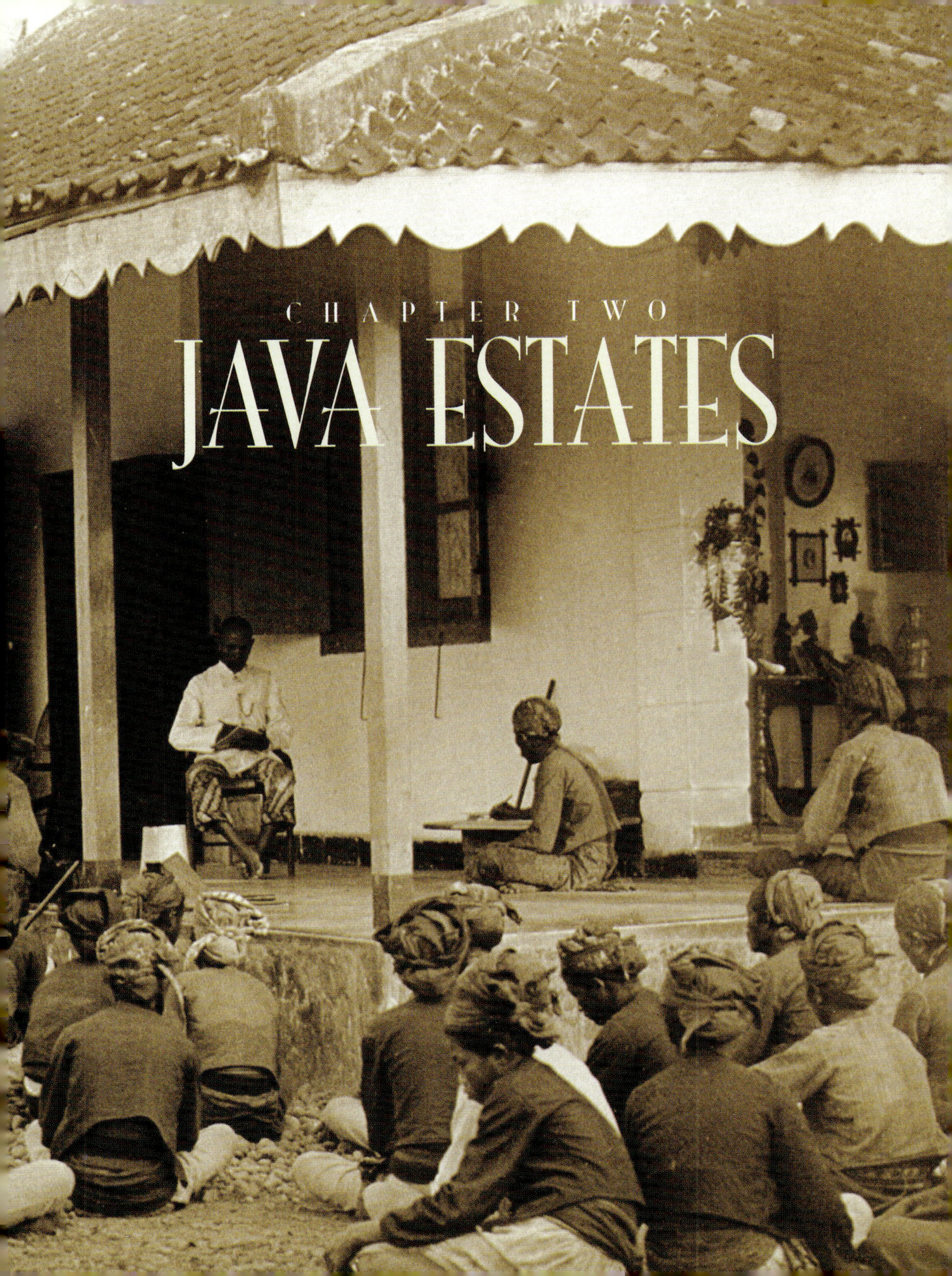

Two key factors mark the history of coffee cultivation on the island of Java. The first was the cultivation system which forced peasants to grow coffee all over Java on what became massive government plantations. The second was the rust disease of 1880 which destroyed nearly all the arabica plants on the island and prompted Indonesia to plant the resistant robusta variety. Today one can find over one hundred private and government plantations scattered along the slopes of the volcanoes in a thousand-kilometer chain that runs the entire length of Java. Most of the coffee is grown by smallholders who sell their beans to traders, who in turn sell it on to roasting companies. Most of the coffee grown is still the inferior robusta variety, although several planters still harvest arabica. In this chapter we take a look at some of the more venerable plantations that Java has to offer.

◂ *Steaming cups of Java coffee* ▴ *A seventy-kilogram bag of world-class Java Coffee Jampit*
◂◂ *A meeting with plantation employees at the Djombor Indigo and Coffee Estate near Sukoardjo, ca. 1920*

PT PN XII – 1896

Of all coffee cultivated on the island of Java, there is one type that is renowned around the world: Estate Java. Essentially, Estate Java coffee is arabica grown on the four estates managed by the Indonesian government: Blawan (2487 hectares), Jampit (1483 ha), Pancoer (400 ha) and Kayumas (412 ha). All these estates are tucked into the hills of Mt. Ijen on the eastern corner of Java, 900 to 1600 meters above sea level. These estates are owned and operated by PT PN XII (Perusahaan Terbatas Perkebunan Nusantara XII or State Plantation Number 12), and current annual production is around four thousand tonnes of green coffee beans.

Most state-owned enterprises in Indonesia are renowned for their suffocating bureaucracy and poor quality product. Not so with PT PN XII. The management has thankfully been allowed to run the company nearly free of interference from Jakarta and today produces some of the finest arabicas in the world.

A label from one variety of Starbucks coffee, and an example of the popularity of Estate Java
Unripened coffee cherries · *The guest house on the Jampit Estate, dating back to the Dutch era*

All these estates were established in the late 1800s by the government of the Netherlands East Indies. After Indonesia declared independence in 1945, these four plantations were nationalized by the new government. Estate Java has enjoyed a popular and dedicated following overseas, with eighty-five percent of its unroasted beans exported to Europe, the United States and Japan.

Once any ripe coffee beans ("cherries") are picked from the coffee tree, they are processed by either the washed (wet process) or unwashed (dry process) method. All Estate Java beans are treated using the wet process, where the pulp of the cherry is separated from the bean after being washed in a labyrinth of free-flowing water. More common on smaller plantations, the dry process involves laying out the cherries in the sun to dry for up to three weeks. After the outer skin has been removed, the beans are left to dry in the sun or placed in drying machines before being graded, bagged and finally sold to roasters.

▲ *Sorting freshly-picked coffee cherries at the Jampit Estate* ▶ *Cherries being washed*
◀◀ *Drying coffee at an estate near Magelang, ca. 1900*

Drying the coffee 127.

Kawisari & Sengon – 1911

To the east of the Estate Java plantations lie other remnants of the Dutch period. Kawisari and Sengon, with a combined area of 880 hectares, were established as Dutch government estates and nationalized by the Indonesian government around 1950. The plantations were slowly privatized in the 1970s and today both are privately owned. Since the altitude of Kawisari and Sengon is slightly lower than that of the Estate Java plantations, the current crop is ninety-five percent robusta with the balance arabica – all of it sold to higher-quality coffee roasters in East Java.

▲ Robusta coffee trees, ca. 1920 ▶ A massive coffee-drying drum on the Kawisari Estate
◀◀ Drying coffee at an estate near Magelang, ca. 1900

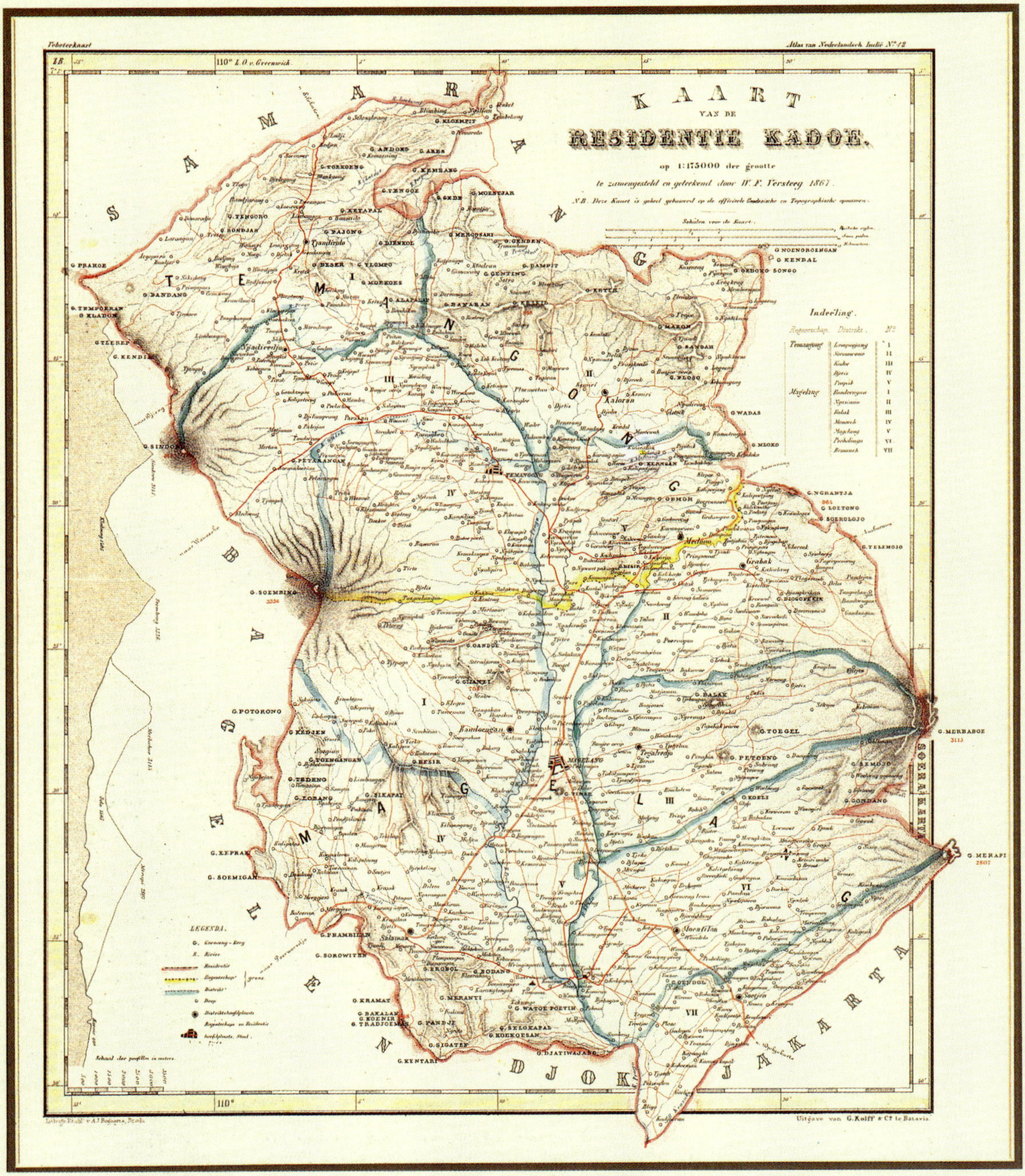
Atlas van Nederlandsch Indië No. 12
KAART
VAN DE
RESIDENTIE KADOE.
op 1:175000 der grootte
te zamengesteld en geteekend door W. F. Versteeg 1867.
Schalen voor de Kaart.
Indeeling.
SAMARANG
TEMANGGONG
MAGELANG
BAGELEN
DJOKJAKARTA
SOERAKARTA
G. MERBABOE
G. MERAPI
G. SOEMBING
G. SINDORO
Temanggong
Magelang
LEGENDA.
Uitgave van G. Kolff & Co te Batavia.

Losari – 1928

Nestled in the highlands of Central Java stands the Losari Coffee Plantation – Resort and Spa. Today one is greeted by a veritable museum of Javanese architecture with traditional Kudus houses, colonial-era villas and even an authentic Turkish bath. Yet Losari is also surrounded by a twenty-hectare, fully-functioning coffee plantation producing ten tonnes of robusta per year.

In 1922 a young Dutchman, Gustav Van der Swan, leased a total of fourteen hectares from the government of the Netherlands East Indies to start a coffee plantation. At the time this area was relatively unexplored due to its prohibitive – but stunning – mountainous terrain. Indeed, the plantation is located 900 meters above sea level and is surrounded by no fewer than eight volcanoes. He named his

◂ *A map of the area surrounding the Losari Coffee Plantation from 1867*
▴ *A view of Mount Sumbing, one of Losari's eight volcanoes*

estate Karangredjo Coffee Plantation and complemented it with the construction of the plantation manor house in 1928. Van der Swan planted robusta seedlings – production began in earnest in 1932 – and remained proprietor of the plantation through the war and into the first decades of independence. One reason he managed to keep control and avoid nationalization was that he had several wives and the multiple layers of this extended family confused any interested parties.

After forty years in the mountains of Central Java, maintaining a coffee plantation proved too much for the aging Van der Swan. He sold the plantation in 1964 to Colonel Tjokroprawiro, a retired army officer and hero of the revolution from Salatiga. Tjokroprawiro kept cultivating coffee until 1988 when he passed away. His wife took over the day-to-day operations, but, like Van der Swan, maintenance proved too difficult and costly and by 1991 she was ready to find a buyer.

Around this time, Gabriella Teggia was trekking through the mountains looking for some old coffee plantations where she could develop a new concept of resort. Asking around from village to village, she finally met an old man who pointed her in the direction of Karangredjo. Arriving at the manor house, she was immediately taken aback by the beauty of the location, and by the state of disrepair of the plantation and its environs. The plantation hadn't been properly maintained since the death of Tjokroprawiro and the buildings on the premises were in shambles. Undeterred, she set out to find the owner. She purchased the plantation with the help of partner Anita Dewayani on the last day of December 1991. To mark a clear break with the past, they changed the name from Karangredjo to Losari, after the village in which it is located.

▸ *Losari employees removing the dried, outer skin of the coffee beans.*
◂◂ *The restored 1928 manor house, now serving as a library and dining room*

Entering Losari today, one's first stop is the Mayong Train Station. Mayong was built in 1878 in the regency of Jepara – 150 kilometers away. It is at Losari now, thanks to the quick action of the founding partners. When they received a phone call from a friend in Semarang, Harry Dasono, telling that this historic station was about to be torn down and sold for its valuable teak, the partners dashed to the owners, PT Kereta Api, and the Indonesian authorities. They asked for and got permission to transport the station and restore it on the grounds of Losari. Under the cover of darkness the entire station was disassembled, loaded on ten lorries and shipped to Losari for preservation.

The Mayong Train Station isn't the only architectural treasure rescued by Losari. In 2002 the partners got another phone call – this time from a friend in Kudus – warning that three *Rumah Adat Kudus* (traditional

A bag of Losari coffee *The Mayong Train Station greets all visitors as they enter Losari*
The Queen of the Mountain cog-wheel steam train, soon to be reunited with the Losari Coffee Plantation

LOSARI
LOSARI
LOSARI
AA 9341 LB
ISUZU
ISUZU

Kudus-style houses with ornate carvings) were about to meet a similar fate. The owners wanted a more modern-looking house made from concrete rather than wood and had begun to sell the antique teak, piece by piece. So the Losari partners rushed to Kudus. After a full day of negotiations, they struck a deal with the owners and shipped the three houses to Losari. The partners' fascination with *pesisir* architecture, from the northern coast of Java, began over twenty years ago and these Kudus houses were to become the Losari's crown jewels.

It is not just the architectural heritage that has been secured at Losari. Using traditional structures and techniques, the Losari team – now an eclectic mix of both local and foreign owners – have resurrected the traditional *joglo* and *limasan* housing styles, to create a plantation as well as a resort like no other in the entire archipelago.

▲ *The coffee shop in the early morning*
◂ *Bags of Losari coffee being taken to the local market*

MBO
PIDJIEOMBO
GB
2

Rawaseneng – 1953

It is generally accepted that coffee was first cultivated and brewed in Ethiopia and later Yemen at the Sufi monastery founded by the "Saint of Mocha", Ali bin Omar al-Shadili. A fascinating contemporary parallel to this story is a little-known Trappist monastery located on a coffee plantation in Rawaseneng, Central Java.

The Our Lady of St. Maria Monastery was founded on 1 April 1953 and was the first Trappist monastery in Indonesia. It was built on an existing coffee plantation first operated by a German named Ernest Heinrich Eisner. When Eisner died in 1930, he left the entire plantation to the parish of St. Aloysius in Semarang, which in turn founded an agricultural school on the premises. After several years, the Bishop of Batavia asked the parish of St. Aloysius to begin preparations for the establishment of Indonesia's first Trappist monastery.

During the Japanese occupation of 1942-1945, the Imperial Army seized the plantation and appointed one of its officers, Heida, to manage it. Apparently plantation skills were in short supply in the Imperial Army and consequently Heida ran the plantation into the ground and nearly destroyed the entire 315 hectares of coffee plants.

When the Japanese surrendered in 1945, representatives of St. Aloysius went to the plantation only to discover that members of the Indonesian rebel army had occupied it and now refused to budge. By 1950 they finally ceded control but burned all the buildings when they left. The same year Brother Bavo van der Ham, a monk from the Tilburg Monastery in Holland, came to Indonesia as the advance team for establishing the monastery. The plantation and its buildings were in ruins so Brother Bavo hired L.E. Mende, a Catholic from Manado, to manage the plantation and restore it to its former

◂ Father Sebastian on a tour of Rawaseneng's three-hundred-hectare coffee plantation
◂◂ Packing bags of coffee at the Pidgie Ombo Estate in Malang, East Java, ca. 1915

productive state. In 1953 the second team of monks came from Tilburg (Baldinus, Nicasius, Sylvester and Maurus) and on 1 April the Cistercian Monastery of Our Lady of St. Maria Rawaseneng was officially opened as a chapter of the central monastery in Tilburg.

Gradually more young people joined the order and on 26 December 1958 Rawaseneng monastery became an autonomous priory. Unfortunately this period of relative calm for the monastery came to a sudden halt in 1965 when members of the Indonesian Communist Party (Partai Komunis Indonesia – PKI) 'nationalized' half the plantation. They destroyed the coffee trees to plant cassava and corn, leaving St. Maria with 176 hectares. There was a real risk that the monastery would continue to be victimized so, on 1 January 1966, St. Aloysius formally requested protection of the Indonesian army.

Major Ngaspin Sugiarjo was assigned to protect the monks and the plantation. Unfortunately he seized the opportunity to not only take the entire production off the hands of the monks but also to nationalize their coffers over the course of the next year. It wasn't until 1 April 1967 that the management of the plantation was returned to the monks of St. Maria. They have been running the monastery and the plantation ever since.

▲ *Baskets of fresh Rawaseneng coffee*
▶ *Early days in the monastery*

Besides coffee, the monastery has over one hundred head of dairy cattle which produce fresh milk for the entire community. There are thirty monks at present, and the last remaining monk of the original delegation, Father Maurus, oversees milk production and makes traditional gouda cheese for visitors.

Like nearly all plantations in Central Java its beans are robusta. The monastery produces sixty tonnes per year and sells it under the brand "Rawaseneng". All of its 130 full-time employees come from the neighboring villages, and the monastery's troubled past seems laid to rest.

▲ *One of the monastery's dairy cows*
▶ *Sorting and grading the coffee beans*

EERSTE WELTEVREDENSCHE KOFFIEBRANDERIJ
GELD
LOTERY

CHAPTER THREE

JAVA ROAST

The other half of the coffee-making process takes place when the green coffee beans leave the plantation. While top-quality raw ingredients are vital to ensure a good cup of Java, some would argue that the real skill and artistry occur in the roasting and blending process. The science of roasting is extremely complex as there are over fifteen hundred different chemical reactions occurring once the beans touch heat. All beans react differently to the heat, and a good roastmaster can pull out subtle flavors hidden within. Since the roasting process is so quick (between eight and fourteen minutes per batch), carelessness on the part of the roaster can destroy beans that have taken hundreds of hours to produce.

Some roasters sell their coffee by the whole bean, but in Indonesia the vast majority sell it as *kopi bubuk*, or powdered coffee. The drink that is made from this powder is called *kopi tubruk* and resembles Turkish coffee. Just add hot water and stir, and be sure to let the grounds settle to the bottom before you drink.

The other responsibility of roasters is marketing the coffee once the beans are roasted. Some will sell their roasted beans to wholesalers, but most prefer to roast, blend, grind and sell the beans themselves. Once beans are roasted they become a perishable product and, if left in warehouses for too long, lose their flavor.

Freshly-roasted arabica coffee beans ready for grinding and brewing
The oldest existing brand of coffee in Indonesia: Tek Sun Ho

PROBAT

Tek Sun Ho – 1878

Every country in the world has its own national or staple brand of coffee. Mention Douwe Egberts to a Dutchman, Lavazza to an Italian, or Maxwell House to an American, and they immediately see a steaming cup of coffee. To an Indonesian, that brand is Tek Sun Ho.

Way back in 1878 Liauw Tek Siong was the proprietor of a food stall on Molenvliet Oost (now named Jalan Hayam Wuruk) in central Batavia. Each day a traveling saleswoman would visit and sell him fresh coffee beans, carried around in a basket on her head. Tek Siong would roast these beans in a small pan and sell them to some of the wealthier residents in this upscale neighborhood. He realized he was selling much more coffee than other items and so bought a small store to focus on selling coffee under his own brand, Tek Sun Ho.

Tek Siong ran his *toko kopi* (coffee store) until 1927 when he handed the daily operations over to his son, Liauw Tian Djie. Tian Djie's first priority was to stop using the roasting pan and to mechanize the process by way of a roasting drum. In 1938, to celebrate the company's 60th anniversary, Tian Djie had a logo designed for his branded coffee, a sketch of the woman who originally sold his father the beans. He also started exporting his roasted beans to the Netherlands. He had three grades of roasted coffee with the lowest one blended with corn to make it affordable to even the poorest residents.

▲ *An original bag of Warung Tinggi coffee featuring the woman who sold Liauw Tek Siong his first coffee beans*
◀ *Master roaster Hendra Widjaja supervising the roasting of Bakoel Koffie's Heritage 1969 blend*

The company continued to expand and the entire family was involved in the roasting business. Shortly after the alleged coup by the Indonesian Communist Party in 1965, the government passed a regulation which prohibited companies from using Chinese names. Tian Djie chose the brand Warung Tinggi, or 'tall shop', as his store was the tallest building in the neighborhood. In 1969 the company's management entered its third generation when his son, Liauw Tiam Yan, took over. Tiam Yan continued with his father's mechanization plans and began packing his beans in aluminium foil instead of brown paper.

The company remained on Hayam Wuruk until 1994 when production outpaced capacity and the roasting machines were moved out to Tangerang, west of Jakarta. By then the company was exporting to Japan, the Middle East and the Netherlands, as well as selling locally though supermarkets. Since the company was growing so rapidly, and so many family members were involved, a decision was made in 2001 to split into two groups: one to continue with the Warung Tinggi brand and the other to establish a new brand called Bakoel Koffie. The famous Warung Tinggi brand was eventually sold to another investor, but Bakoel Koffie remained in the family. It is managed by Hendra and Syenny Widjaja, Liauw Tek Siong's great-grandchildren, ensuring the country's oldest coffee roasting tradition will continue for a long time to come.

▲ ▶ *Bags of Bakoel Koffie and the inside of their café on Jalan Barito in South Jakarta*

Freshly

PREMIUM
GRADE

KOPI
Kapal Api
Kapal Api
SPECIAL
Kapal Api
SPECIAL
Kapal Api
SPECIAL
Kapal Api
Kapal Api

Kapal Api – 1927

Kapal Api's founder, Go Soe Loet, started operations in 1927. He came from Fujian province in China to Indonesia in the early part of the century. By instinct he was a trader and while selling vegetables in the market he noticed great numbers of people drinking coffee. He decided to enter this business and sold his coffee under the brand Kapal Api, or 'steam ship', after the vessel that brought him to the shores of the Netherlands East Indies.

As was common at the time, Soe Loet would blend his coffee with corn to keep the price down, a practice which still takes place today. Several companies sold coffee but in the Netherlands East Indies most of the coffee was unbranded. Until the 1970s, coffee was considered a commodity rather than a specialist product and was sold through traditional markets in hundred-gram packets wrapped in newspaper.

Go Soe Loet's second son, Soedomo Mergonoto, began working in the company in 1968 as a salesman. At that time, production was a few hundred kilos a day and the company was selling its coffee only in Surabaya and its environs. One day, while Soedomo was walking through one of Surabaya's traditional markets he noticed some strange happenings with soap. Traditional merchants were still slicing off individual bars from big blocks. But companies like Unilever were beginning to sell soap in pre-wrapped bars and single-serving packets. Additionally, these foreign companies were advertising – something rarely done by domestic companies.

Following their lead, Soedomo, who took over the top management post in 1978, set his plan in action. He decided to sell his coffee in hundred-gram, individually wrapped packets and to advertise on television. Since he had

◂ *The idea that made Kapal Api the largest coffee roaster in Indonesia: single serving packets*

no marketing budget, he hired freelancers and called in a favor to get one of Surabaya's most famous comedians, Paimo, to appear in the ad. All Paimo did was take a sip of his coffee and say, "This is good coffee." The ad was run two times a week for three months on the local TVRI channel in Surabaya.

The ad was an immediate hit and sales multiplied literally overnight. This small, sleepy company was catapulted from the eighth largest in Surabaya to number one in only three months. Soedomo realized he needed to mechanize and in 1982 he purchased a 500- kilo-per-hour roasting machine from Germany. His dream was that this would be running seven hours a day after a few years. As it turned out, this machine was running twenty-four hours a day only a year later, and by the mid-1980s Kapal Api was the largest coffee company in Indonesia.

Until this time Kapal Api was just a coffee roasting company with no plantations of its own. In 1986, the Indonesian government approached the company with an offer: in exchange for ownership of an old Dutch coffee plantation on Mount Kalossi in Central Sulawesi, Kapal Api would promise to develop the area. Since then the company has built twenty-six bridges and hundreds of kilometers of roads. The company is also implementing a sharecropper scheme in which peasants have the right to farm the land and then sell the coffee beans to the company at market price.

A visit to Kapal Api today finds not only its original 500-kilo-per-hour machine still in use, but also the largest roasting machine in the world with the capacity to roast five tonnes an hour. Kapal Api also has one of the country's most efficient distribution companies taking its coffee to each and every one of Indonesia's provinces.

▲ *The comedian Paimo in one of Kapal Api's print advertisements*
◀ *A steaming glass of Kapal Api's* kopi bubuk

Singa – 1928

One year after the founding of Kapal Api, another Go in Surabaya started his own coffee roasting company, although Go See Pwe's vision was slightly different. From the beginning See Pwe sold his coffee under the brand Singa ('lion') in and around Surabaya. As there were few branded products at that time, the reputation of Singa grew quickly and all around Surabaya the lion logo was a familiar sight.

Go's son, See Tjeng, took over the reigns of the company in the 1940s and kept with his father's tradition of selling the highest quality by blending the coffee himself, and by remaining focused on the Surabaya market.

The company's management entered its third generation in the 1970s when See Tjeng's son, Biantoro Sudargo took over. He began the process of mechanizing the company with the purchase of Brazilian roasting machines, and beefed up the company's distribution outside of Surabaya. Furthermore, Biantoro began buying beans from outside Java, in particular from Toraja. Focusing on the upper market segment, Biantoro also sensed opportunities among the less well-heeled. In the 1990s, he began to reach the mass market by developing coffee premixed with sugar and creamer. Although not labeled as such, their blend of arabica coffee contains beans from PT PN XII, the plantation that produces the famed Estate Java coffee.

▲ *The latest design for Singa's arabica coffee*

AROMA – 1930

Nestled on a side street in the frantic center of Bandung lies one of Indonesia's most renowned coffee roasters: Aroma Koffie Fabriek. The clamor of street hawkers and electronic stores suddenly disappears once one steps through the narrow wood-paneled doors into the aroma of fresh roasted coffee. Here is a place which evokes an era long feared lost.

Since 1930, when Tan Houw Sian opened his coffee store on Jalan Banceuy, very little has changed. The German roasting machine is dated 1936, the beans are still purchased from all over Indonesia and aged an average of seven years, and the owner still personally roasts the beans each morning. The only real change is probably the owner himself, the son of Tan Houw Sian, Widyapratama or Pak Widya for short.

Pak Widya took over daily operations from his father in 1971 and proudly claims that he has never taken a day off from the business. He still follows his father's custom of selecting the best beans from farmers all over the archipelago from Aceh to East Java to Timor, as well as resisting calls to open up a café. He's keeping focused on his main business: roasting quality coffee.

▸ *The original bag of Aroma coffee*

▴ *"Once tried, always desired" – Aroma's old label in Dutch*

DIEDRICH

Caswell's – 2000

Growing up in Boston, Henry Harmon enjoyed the reputation of having the mother who always made a good cup of coffee. Neighbors would find a reason to drop by the Harmon house just to try some of his mom's famous coffee. A half-century later and halfway around the world, Henry is continuing this tradition of making fine coffee for guests.

The most recent addition to Java's fine roasters is Caswell's Coffee which began operations in early 2000. The founder, Henry Harmon, had been running a specialty grocery store in South Jakarta called Caswell's Mom's when he noticed he was getting more and more requests from his customers for fine Indonesian coffee. As is the case for most of Indonesia's fine products, from paper to furniture to coffee, the highest quality is always exported to developed countries where it fetches higher prices than in the domestic market. Even the famous Estate Javas were better known – and more accessible – in the cafés of Seattle than in Jakarta. So Henry decided to do something

▲ *A cupping session for the roasts of the day at Caswell's*
◀ *Caswell's top-of-the-range Diedrich roasting machine*

about it. He purchased a roaster from Diedrich Roasters in the United States and attended seminars hosted by the Specialty Coffee Association of America to learn the intricacies of roasting and blending. He came back to Jakarta and worked with his roasters to develop profiles for each of his single-origin coffee beans, a process that took six months.

His roasters have designed three signature blends: Archipelago, Blend #3 and of course the oldest blend of them all, Mocha-Java. Curiously Caswell's is one of the few places in Indonesia where you can get a cup of pure Estate Java coffee. These beans are exported to the United States, and then brought home via Atlas Coffee Importers in Seattle, USA.

Going one step further in the specialty coffee business, Henry has also trained his *baristas* (coffee makers) in the little-known area of "latté art" and one of them, *mbak* Siti, actually won the Asian Barista Championship held in 2002 in Kuala Lumpur.

▲ *A perfect example of Caswell's "latté art"*
▸ *A gunnybag full of unroasted Estate Java coffee beans*

CASWELL'S COFFEE
ountry of Origin: INDONESIA
of Coffee: JAVA ESTATE
This is standard by which coffee is measured. Java's finest golden bean, yields strong vibrant flavor, a rich full body, and low acidity.

500

CHAPTER FOUR

JAVA JIVE

Fly to Java
by
K.N.I.L.M.
ROYAL NETHERLANDS INDIES AIRWAYS

I love coffee, I love tea,
I love the java jive and it loves me
Coffee and tea and the jivin' and me,
A cup, a cup, a cup, a cup, a cup!

These lyrics are from the Ink Spot's popular song from the 1940s, Java Jive. Coffee on Java is consumed in more ways and has more uses than is usually imagined. From religious offerings to body scrubs, coffee is more than just a drink on Java. In this chapter we explore the different ways in which coffee is consumed on Java – from the *kraton* to the *kampung* and every *kota* in between.

▲ *The Java Jive coffee shop in Atlanta, Georgia*
◀ *A promotional poster for the Royal Netherlands East Indies Airline Company, ca. 1930*
◀◀ *A Java market scene selling unbranded coffee the traditional way by price per hundred-gram servings*

Java in the Kraton

Most visitors to Indonesia are told the country is ninety per cent Muslim, but what cannot be overlooked is that Java (Central and East), while embracing Islam, is one hundred per cent Javanese. This is important as the Javanese constitute the single biggest ethnic group in Southeast Asia. And while eighty-five per cent adhere to Islam, it is an Islam with a strong overlay of Javanese-ness called *kejawen*. In Central Java this body of ritual and belief is centered on the royal courts of Solo and Yogyakarta, while in East Java it is centered around the *pesantren* (Islamic boarding schools) that speckle the countryside. It is *kejawen* which gives a Javanese directions for living, through rituals steeped in mysticism dating back thousands of years.

For example, twice a week, on Tuesdays and Thursdays, an offering is made to Kyai Petruk, a Muslim preacher, to protect the formal dining room of the *kraton* royal palace in Solo. The offering

▲ *A porcelain coffee cup from the private collection of the* Susuhunan *of Solo*
◂ *A servant in the Solo* kraton *making an offering with incense, tea and coffee to Kyai Petruk*

always includes white rose petals, incense and coffee. Kyai Petruk is the guardian spirit of Mount Merapi as well as the protector of the dining room. This dining room, named Sasana Andrawina, is still used today for state dinners. Coffee has featured in these offerings as a nectar for the gods ever since the time of Ali al-Shadili. It is used to bring enlightenment and a state of otherworldliness. And in Solo, otherworldliness is one of the founding tenets of the *kraton*.

Outside the palace there is another event where coffee plays a central role. During the *kirab pusaka*, or celebration of the Javanese New Year, sacred buffalo are fed bananas and coffee before the ceremony begins. Historically, this ritual was only practiced when a plague or other hardship befell the community, but when President Suharto came to power in 1965, he ordered that it be practiced every year.

▲ Kraton *guards preparing coffee for the sacred buffalo*

▶ *The* Susuhunan *of Solo, Pakoe Boewono XII, enjoying a cup of coffee after a state dinner in the Solo* kraton

DILARANG NAIK
DON'T STEP ON IT

In the courts of Yogyakarta, coffee is consumed slightly differently. For example, while most regard coffee itself as a suitably effective stimulant, the guards of the *kraton* actually add salt to their coffee. Some believe the mixing of salt with caffeine gives that added hit so necessary in the tropics, particularly when one is numbed by the smoking of *kretek* cigarettes. Others wonder if the salt is meant to replace that which is lost by sweating under the heavy ceremonial garb of the palace.

The coffee cups of the *kraton* feature illustrations of members of the royal family, pressed under a delicate glaze. They are considered so sacred they are only allowed to be handled by the personal servants of the Sultan and by the Sultan himself.

▲ *One of the royal coffee cups in the Yogyakarta* kraton ◀ *Servants bringing a special delivery of coffee for Sultan Hamengkoe Boewono X* ◀◀ *The courtyard of the Yogyakarta* kraton

Java in the Kampung

While the Sultan and the *Susuhunan* are the lords of the *kraton*, at the other end of the spectrum is the *kepala desa*. The *kepala desa*, or village head, is the one who holds the moral authority in the village and the one who hears all the problems afflicting the villagers. Once a month, the men in the village will sit cross-legged in a room, the obligatory cup of coffee in front of them, with the *kepala desa* listening and then offering his advice.

Disputes range from missing goats to missing wives and it is the responsibility of the *kepala desa* to maintain peace and harmony among the villagers. The ideal for each village is summed up by *toto tentrem kerto rahardjo*, which literally means 'ordered, established and secure well-being'. The *kepala desa*'s responsibility is to maintain this ideal in his capacity as a spiritual leader first and as an administrator second. Such harmony is considered vital to every village and if it is disrupted then inevitably problems will occur.

▲ *Pouring cups of coffee* ▶ *The* kepala desa *and members of the village discussing recent events* ◀◀ *A typical coffee stall near Salatiga, Central Java*

LIMBOTO SEDIA
ES JERUK
TEH MANIS
KOPI SUSU
KOPI MANIS
BERITA KOTA

WARUNG KOPI
SEDIA INDOMI REBUS/GORENG
ROTI BAKAR
ES TEH MANIS
KOPI MANIS
ES JERUK
KOPI SUSU
SUSU ZODAH

As the men gather to solve the village's problems, the women get together in support groups and engage in a different social dynamic called *arisan*. An *arisan* is a loose grouping of women of the same ethnic group or background who gather once a month to discuss their family's problems, gossip about other groups, or just share a new recipe.

The other role of an *arisan* is as a combination of a community savings and loan center and a lucky draw: each member puts an agreed amount of money into a pot each month and numbers are drawn to see who will be buying the new dress or television set that month. As with meetings with the *kepala desa*, glasses of *kopi tubruk* are considered an essential part of this gathering.

Preparing the coffee for the monthly arisan *meeting*

The well-known warung kopi *('coffee stall') found all over the island of Java*

In the village of Grabag, Central Java, a different kind of monthly meeting is held. This one is for the younger men in the area who gather to drink coffee and show off their customized motor scooters. The Grabag Vespa Club began in the early 1990s and currently has twenty members. After downing a cup of coffee, the riders head off around the neighboring villages ostensibly to show off their new vehicles, but invariably to create situations which will be debated at the next meeting with the *kepala desa*.

▲ *The Grabag Vespa Club gearing up, and*
◂ *riding through a village near the Losari Coffee Plantation.*

Among the less fortunate folk in the villages – those who savor a cup of Java but can't afford it – a special kind of coffee is consumed. *Teh Tiungka* is neither tea nor coffee, but a combination of the two. Freshly-picked coffee leaves are roasted over an open flame and then boiled in water to make a coffee-flavored tea. Another low-cost option is coffee mixed with corn. *Kopi jagung*, as it is called, is most commonly found in North Sumatra these days, but until recently it was found all over Java. This is not as strange as it might sound – in the 19th century the French would add chicory to their coffee powder, Americans added egg yolks and the British would roast their beans in butter.

▲ *Glasses of* kopi jagung *– coffee mixed with corn*
▶ *Boiling freshly-picked coffee leaves to make* Teh Tiungka *– coffee-flavored tea*

arOmas
morning

Java in the Kota

From Jakarta to Surabaya one can find cafés in nearly every city and town. Some are the familiar and unpretentious *warung kopi* ('coffee stall') and some are the more upmarket and decidedly elegant cafés. Only recently, however, Western-style chains have begun opening outlets in urban areas – witness the recently built Cilandak Town Square in South Jakarta where there are no fewer than seven cafés in a ten-meter radius.

While Western-style chains like Starbucks and the Coffee Club are surely a welcome addition to the city's coffee scene, it is surprising that they were not the first to enter the upper-market café segment. That honor goes to home-grown Excelso, which opened its first café in Jakarta's Plaza Indonesia in 1991. Excelso, a unit of Kapal Api, has expanded to thirty-six cafés and distributes its coffee beans through grocery stores all over the archipelago.

An upmarket café in Solo, Central Java ▲ *Have a cup of Java coffee in Java Kafe, Yogyakarta*
A typical urban café scene at Bakoel Koffie, South Jakarta

MYSTIC JAVA

Ever since coffee was discovered, it has been considered mystical and its use in Indonesia is no different. For example, in the holy Menoreh Hills on the Kedu Plains, there are several sacred tombs of warriors where offerings are made. As legend tells it, before battle the warriors would go on mystic retreats and pray to the gods for protection in battle. These days the coffee and incense offerings are made not just to the gods but also to the warriors themselves.

Another contemporary use of coffee is in trance dances. A dancer will eat coffee leaves, mysteriously fall into an hypnotic state and become a form of spiritual medium where he is able to perform extraordinary feats like eating glass and walking on burning coconut husks. These mediums apparently convey messages from the spirits – including which particular kind of coffee they prefer in their offerings.

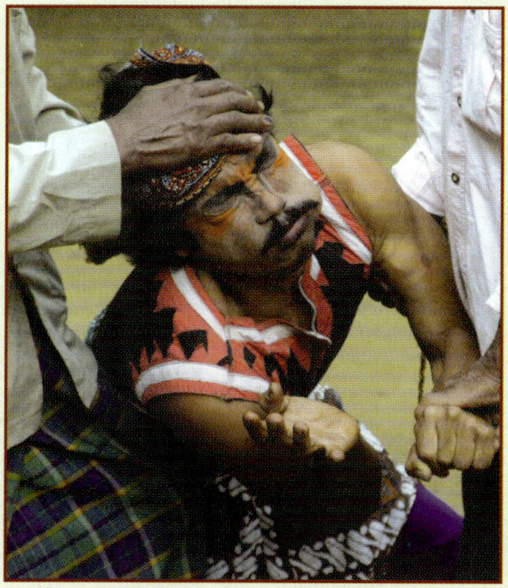

A trance dancer receiving messages from the spirits
An offering of coffee is made in the Menoreh Hills of Central Java.
The temple of Borobudur at the base of the mystical Menoreh Hills

Java Curiosities

Although most coffee in Java is intended for drinking, there are many curious uses for coffee that are less well known. For example, a 1934 Dutch botanical encyclopedia claimed that "roasted coffee is a good disinfectant to be sprinkled under and around corpses" and "to keep roses and other plants free of insects sprinkle coffee grounds on the soil." In contemporary society, it has uses ranging from hair dye to paint for elaborate designs on cigarettes (*ce te* painting in Kediri), and from Java coffee scrub in massages to the *kopi pecah*, or broken coffee, *batik* pattern.

More subtle is the evolving role of coffee as a social symbol. What kind of coffee one drinks, and how, is as much an indicator of class on Java as it is anywhere else. Individualists in the West might see fresh-ground, individually-tailored coffee as a sign of sophistication. But in rural Java it is the processed Nescafé which proclaims an up-and-coming consumer. A startling but common sight, often in the same areas which produce some of the world's most impressive coffees, is the aspiring middle class Javanese proudly tearing open a plastic sachet, while the tourist begs for *kopi tubruk*. In the urban areas, the better established are using espresso machines at home or buying lattés in the malls.

As Indonesians rediscover the richness of tastes, flavors and styles offered by their home-grown coffee industry, the age-old demand for a cup of Java is still growing. By demanding high quality beans and roasts, new generations of coffee-lovers are helping to enrich a tradition developed on Java centuries ago.

◂ *A Javanese woman eschews the plastic sachet in favor of a fresh, hot glass of* kopi tubruk
◂◂ *A tarpaulin with a coffee pot and cup used to shield a* warung kopi *from the sun.*
▸▸ *Contemporary uses for coffee: a body scrub, a* batik *pattern, and an ingredient in recipes*

APPENDICES

KOPI LUWAK

No book on coffee in Java would be complete without mentioning perhaps the strangest coffee of all, *kopi luwak*.

The legend is as follows: civet cats (*luwak*) known for roaming the archipelago have a penchant for the best coffee beans around. So they eat the beans straight from the coffee bush and, failing to digest them, pass them out in their feces intact. *Kopi luwak* harvesters claim the honour of collecting those beans and roasting a cup of coffee like no other. The digestive tract of the civet cat is the most unusual known incubator of coffee beans. The civet (*pictured left*) supposedly eats the reddest, ripest coffee cherries on the tree, and the beans emerge still wrapped in the cherry's mucilage.

We say legend, because after months of research we're frankly not convinced. We have failed to find any coffee-seller who admits to actually collecting *kopi luwak* from the feces of the civet cat. To them, the term *kopi luwak* nowadays means simply the beans which the *luwak* or civet cat would choose to eat, that is, beans of the highest quality.

Trading on imagery is hardly new. *Kopi luwak* sellers are hoping the legend of the civet cat's taste buds assures consumers that they are enjoying the best beans around. Retail prices overseas hover around the US$100 per pound mark, at least, so legends come at a price. On Java, mysticism comes second to harsh reality, and the same amount of *kopi luwak* sells for under a dollar.

FOR FURTHER READING

Allen, Stewart Lee *The Devil's Cup: Coffee, the Driving Force in History* © 1999 Soho Press

Banks, Mary et al *The World Encyclopedia of Coffee* ©1999, 2002 Anness Publishing

Geertz, Clifford *The Religion of Java* ©1960 The Free Press

Hattox, Ralph *Coffee and Coffeehouses: The Origins of a Social Beverage in the Medieval Near East* ©1985 University of Washington Press

Jacob, Heinrich Eduard *Coffee: The Epic of a Commodity* Trans. Eden and Cedar Paul © 1935 Viking Press

Koentjaraningrat *Javanese Culture* © 1985 Oxford University Press

Liss, David *The Coffee Trader* © 2003 Abacus Books

Mulder, Niels *Mysticism in Java* ©1998 The Pepin Press

Pendergast, Mark *Uncommon Grounds: The History of Coffee and How it Transformed Our World* ©1999 Basic Books

Perry, Sara *The New Complete Coffee Book* ©2001 Chronicle Books

Stella, Alain *The Book of Coffee* ©1996 Flammarion

Wright, Arnold *Twentieth Century Impressions of Netherlands India* ©1909 Lloyd's Greater Britain Publishing Company, Ltd.

INDEX OF NAMES AND PLACES

P.T. BINTANG
PAKAI

ACKNOWLEDGEMENTS

When I was a little girl growing up in Rome, my father would take me out for a walk every Sunday morning. We would stroll through the city's narrow streets to his favorite *caffé*. While he would chat with the other customers buying their morning espresso, I would quietly stand in the corner and absorb the din of the roasting machine and the aroma of the freshly-roasted beans.

My favorite place was amongst the gunny bags – which were as tall as I was – and once I slipped my finger in one marked "JAVA". I pried out one dark, oily bean which slipped through my fingers and onto the floor. I picked it up and placed the bean in my mouth. My father, who had been keeping his eye on me the entire time, burst out into laughter. He knelt down next to me and lovingly explained, "Dear Gabriella, you aren't supposed to eat coffee – you are supposed to drink it!" He then placed a few drops of his espresso on a sugar cube and placed it on my tongue. At that moment I instinctively realized that my relationship with coffee would be anything but fleeting, but I didn't know then that I would be writing a book not only about coffee but also about this island – and its people – which I have come to adore.

As my father was the first person to introduce me to Java coffee, it is appropriate to acknowledge him first and foremost. There have been many, many other people who have contributed not only to the production of this book, but also to the Losari Coffee Plantation, a few of whom I and my co-author, Mark Hanusz, would like to mention:

Firstly, we would like to express our sincerest thanks to the early supporters of this book: Toeti Heraty, Anna Bambang Sunindar, Ratih and Dr. Subroto, Nono Makarim, Adjie and Asmoro Damais, Maya Moeljadi,

Anita Dewayani, Alessandro, Daniela and Claudia Gazzini, Pietro, Francesco and Riccardo Scalzitti, Andrea Magnaghi, Gianni and Daniela Predieri, Toni Tack, Theodoor Bakker, Ita Budhi, Laksmi Djuwita, Ted Sulisto, Warwick Purser, Ardiyanto, Joop Ave, Jacob Termansen, Takashi Ichiki, Eric Oey, and Vaudine England.

We would also like to acknowledge our deep appreciation to the government of Central Java, in particuliar Bapak Gubernur H. Mardiyanto, Hengky Hermantoro of the Central Java Tourism Bureau, as well as to the Bupati of Magelang, Bapak Drs. H. Hasyim Afandi.

During our arduous photoshoot, we were generously supported by all the members of Casagrande, in particuliar Rully Zulkarnain, Ramli from the Sheraton Mustika Yogyakarta, and Sean Flakelar of Amanjiwo.

Thanks also to those from the Java coffee community who lent their expertise, advice and images: Father Sebastian, Father Maurus, and all the monks of the Rawaseneng Monastery, Windiari Widyastuti of Tlogo, Miftakul Kirom of AEKI, Michel Anhar of Kawisari and Sengon, Soedomo Mergonoto and Pranoto Soenarto of Kapal Api, Henry Harmon and team at Caswell's Coffee, Syenny and Hendra Widjaya and Judith Cook of Bakoel Koffie, Sam Filiaci, Biantoro and Pujiono Sudargo of Singa, Soekarno and Agustono of PTPN XII.

Lastly, we'd like to acknowledge those who provided support in one way or another during the production of this book: KP Aryo Hardjonegoro, KP Eddy S. Wirabhumi, KP Haryo Wironegoro, Gusti Kanjeng Ratu Pembayun, Lam Ngo of KITLV, Helen West of AOTO, Rob Pearce, Hoggi Wahyu and Trisnawaty Sutanto, John Hanusz, James de Rave, Christine Chung, Scott Merrillees, Philip Yampolsky, Bartele Santema, Ken Conboy, Patrick Kavanagh, and the staff of Losari Coffee Plantation and Equinox Publishing.

Gabriella Teggia and Mark Hanusz
Losari, July 2003

PHOTO CREDITS

Page 2 Isabella Ginanneschi, 4 courtesy Gabriella Teggia, 6 courtesy Illinois State Library, 8, 9 Isabella Ginanneschi, 10-11 Michael Sutter, 12-13 KIT, 14 KITLV, 15, 16 private collection, 17 AOTO, 18-19 KIT, 20 private collection, 21 Mark Hanusz, 22-23 KIT, 24 KITLV, 26-27 KIT, 28 private collection, 29, 30-31 KIT, 32 KITLV, 33 private collection, 34-35 KITLV, 37 Isabella Ginanneschi, 38-39 KITLV, 40 Isabella Ginanneschi, 41 Rob Pearce, 42 Isabella Ginanneschi, 43 (*top*) private collection, (*bottom*) courtesy PT PN XII, 44-45 KITLV, 46 courtesy PT PN XII, 47 Isabella Ginanneschi, 48-49 AOTO, 50 KIT, 51 Isabella Ginanneschi, 52 courtesy Theo Bakker, 53-57 Isabella Ginanneschi, 58 (*top*) courtesy Losari Coffee Plantation, (*bottom*) Isabella Ginanneschi, 59-61 Isabella Ginanneschi, 62-63 KITLV, 64, 66 Isabella Ginanneschi, 67 courtesy Rawaseneng, 68 Rob Pearce, 69 Isabella Ginanneschi, 70-72 courtesy Bakoel Koffie, 73 Isabella Ginanneschi, 74 courtesy Bakoel Koffie, 75, 76 private collection, 77 courtesy Bakoel Koffie, 78 Deny Salman, 80 Isabella Ginanneschi, 81 courtesy Kapal Api, 82 courtesy Singa, 83 courtesy Aroma, 84, 85 Rob Pearce, 86 Mark Hanusz, 87 Rob Pearce, 88-89 Isabella Ginanneschi, 90 courtesy Philip Yampolsky, 91 John Hanusz/ Brian McAdams, 92-105 Isabella Ginanneschi, 106-107 Rob Pearce, 108-113 Isabella Ginanneschi, 114-115 Rob Pearce, 116-131 Isabella Ginanneschi, 132-133 Rob Pearce, 134 Isabella Ginanneschi, 135 private collection, 137-143 Isabella Ginanneschi.

KIT – Koninklijk Instituut voor de Tropen, Amsterdam
KITLV – Koninklijk Instituut vor Taal-, Land- en Volkenkunde, Leiden
AOTO - Antiques of the Orient, Singapore

Also from Equinox Publishing

KRETEK: The Culture and Heritage of Indonesia's Clove Cigarettes
By Mark Hanusz
ISBN 979-95898-0-0 **Size** 24.5x32x2.5 cm **Weight** 1.7 kg
Pages 224 **Format** Hardcover

Tales from Djakarta
By Pramoedya Ananta Toer
ISBN 979-95898-1-9 **Size** 14.7x21x2 cm **Weight** 400 g
Pages 288 **Format** Softcover

It's Not An All Night Fair
By Pramoedya Ananta Toer
ISBN 979-95898-2-7 **Size** 14.7x21x.7 cm **Weight** 180 g
Pages 128 **Format** Softcover

The King, the Witch and the Priest
By Pramoedya Ananta Toer
ISBN 979-95898-3-5 **Size** 12.5x19x1 cm **Weight** 150 g
Pages 128 **Format** Softcover

NO REGRETS
Reflections of a Presidential Spokesman
By Wimar Witoelar
ISBN 979-95898-4-3 **Size** 10.5x17.5x1.2 cm **Weight** 250 g
Pages 200 **Format** Softcover

GUS DUR: The Authorized Biography of Abdurrahman Wahid
By Greg Barton
ISBN 979-95898-5-1 **Size** 23x15.3x2.4 cm **Weight** 600 g
Pages 436 **Format** Softcover

TIMOR: A Nation Reborn
by Bill Nicol
ISBN 979-95898-6-X **Size** 15.3x23x3 cm **Weight** 450 g
Pages 352 **Format** Softcover

Jakarta Inside Out
By Daniel Ziv
ISBN 979-95898-7-8 **Size** 17x22x1.2 cm **Weight** 500 g
Pages 184 **Format** Softcover

KOPASSUS: Inside Indonesia's Special Forces
By Ken Conboy
ISBN 979-95898-8-6 **Size** 15x22x2.2 cm **Weight** 400 g
Pages 352 **Format** Softcover

www.equinoxpublishing.com